Inspired by
A. A. Milne

Winnie-the-Pooh's ABC

with illustrations by
Ernest H. Shepard

Dutton Children's Books
New York

Published in the United States by Dutton Children's Books,
a division of Penguin USA
375 Hudson Street
New York, New York 10014

Designed by Joseph Rutt

Printed in Hong Kong
First Edition
ISBN 0-525-45365-2
10 9 8 7 6

A a

apple

B b

balloon

C c

cow

D d

dragon

E e

Eeyore

F f

forest

G g

gate

H h

honey

I i

island

J j

jump

K k

Kanga

L l

lion

M m

mirror

N n

North Pole

O o

Owl

P p

Piglet

Q q

queen

R r

Rabbit

S s

stairs

T t

Tigger

U u

umbrella

V v

violets

W w

Winnie-the-Pooh

X x

e**x**potition

Y y

yellow daffodils

Z z

zoo